Little… I Won't Stay

Cheyenne Lane

BookLeaf Publishing

Presentation by *BookLeaf Publishing*

Web: www.bookleafpub.com

E-mail: info@bookleafpub.com

ISBN: 978-93-95784-52-8

First edition 2022

DEDICATION

To Jaxon and Jace

ACKNOWLEDGEMENT

I want to thank my boys for always having me think outside the box and see everything from a different perspective. Thank you for teaching me and learning with me as we go through life together.

PREFACE

Exploring the world through the perspective of a child. All my poems have came from personal experiences with my 2 boys.

Watch Me Grow

Little… I won't stay.
Just be patient. Watch me play.
I'm learning new things everyday
I'm exploring the world in my own way
Ooo what's that?! What is that sound?!
Ooh look mommy! Look what I found!
Look at me! Look at what I can do!
Hey I can hear you! Can you hear me too?
You're attention I need as I grow.
Just breathe mommy. Be patient, go slow.
Can I show you what excites me?
Ooooo! Do you see that tree?
Fast! Fast! Fast! Run with me!
Watch me count! 1… 2… 3…
I'm learning mommy. I'm watching you.
I want to grow up and be big too!
Yum food! Can I help you cook?
What's wrong? Let me take a look!
I can do it! I am strong!
Mommy will help if something goes wrong.
Wooohooo!! I did it! Did you see?
Look mommy, look! Are you proud of me?
I'm learning with everything I do!
Just go slow mommy. You're learning too!
You show me and I show you.
I'm getting big! Hurray! Woohoo!

Morning routine

2

Wake up in the morning put some slippers on
my feet
My tummy is rumbling, I'm ready to eat
Walk out of my room, good morning mommy!
Into the bathroom because I have to potty
In the bathroom, what do I have to do?
Brush my hair and my teeth too!
Walk to the kitchen, mommy what's to eat?
Cinnamon apple oatmeal? Yum, deliciously
sweet
Off to my room to put on some clothes
I need a shirt, pants, and socks for my toes!
Now I'm dressed and ready for the day
Time to eat, then I can go play

Mommy, help you?

Hey! I hear something!
A lot of banging and thumping
But coming from where?
Sound like the kitchen, I'll head there
And What do I see?
It's mommy cooking!
Ooo mommy, help you? I say looking up
"Of course my baby" she hands me a cup
"Fill it up once with flour then dump in the bowl"
I love helping mommy, I do what I'm told.
She hands me an egg , I crack it in two
I've helped before, I know what to do!
Mommy helps me add milk, then hands me a spoon
All that's left is mixing , we'll be done soon.
In the oven it goes and now we wait
Mommy thanks me for helping and says I did great!
I can't wait to help mommy again
Wonder what we'll be making then.

Playtime!

Jump, jump while I play
Scream loudly with all I say
Running fast! Around and around.
Making toy angels on the ground.
Building towers with my blocks!
What time is it? I can't read clocks.
Bake a cake, ice cream too
What else is there that I can do?
Rock the baby, pet the dog
To the water table with my frog
Shoot a hoop, make the shot
The floor is lava. It's very hot!
Im a doctor! You need care.
Run away! A monster is there.
Line up the cars it's time to race
I'm in an airplane in outer space!
It's time to clean up, play time is done!
We will play again later and have more fun!

Potty Time

Turn on the light. I'm so proud of me!
Now pull down my pants so that I can pee.
Climb on the toilet, let it all out
Hip hip hooray I begin to shout!
Get off the potty, grab some tissue!
Wipe myself clean so I don't have an issue.
Put the tissue in the potty, time to flush
Pull my pants up slowly, I'm not in a rush.
Yay I did it! I'm almost done.
Now washing my hands, the bubbles are fun
Rinse the bubbles off and dry them last
Now turn off the light as I go past
Good job me! I saved the day!
I used the potty! Hip hip hooray!

Blocks

Build a tower very high!
It's so tall it touches the sky!
Oooo look! I made a car.
With these wheels it goes real far!
I love these blocks, they're so fun
Look a purple, blue, and a green one
Colorful blocks all around
Now to spread them on the ground
Look a castle and a boat
I'm making a cow and a goat
My options are endless when I play
I can build blocks all day!

Climb climb climb

I'm an explorer! I must reach the top.
Up mommy mountain, I can not stop!
Over toes, knees and tummies too
Climbing is all I ever do
I climb on shoulders and then your head
I'll climb my way into your bed
Up on a counter or on a shelf
I don't need help, I'll do it myself.
I'm big and brave and strong you see
Watch me mommy as I climb this tree!
I'm the best climber, I can climb so high
You can climb with me just give it a try
There's no place this explorer can't go
I climb high but I also climb low.
Into caves and tunnels, I'll see it all
I'll be really careful so I won't fall
Luckily mommy is always near
With mommy close, I have nothing to fear
I'm an explorer and it's so much fun
Climbing til the day is done.

Car Ride

Mommy said let's go for a car ride
Grabbing my favorite things to go outside
Mommy why cant I bring my bike too
Oh it's too big! I know what to do
I grab my Dino and race car instead
And out to the car is where I head
Down the sidewalk and to the right
Into my seat, mommy buckles me tight
Now we're all in the car and ready to go
Where we are heading I just don't know
Maybe the park? The zoo? The store?
These are some of the places I adore!
Down the road, and past the car
On this trip we go real far!
My eyelids are heavy from all this fresh air.
I'll take a nap, mommy will wake me when
there.

1st Day of School

What is this place? It's new to me.
Ooo look at that! Look what I see.
An octopus, a boat, and a little blue fish
Look it's the cow, moon, spoon, and dish
Do you see humpty dumpy on the wall?
I think this place will be a ball!
Oooo there's more people, look, do you see?
Maybe they can stay and play with me!
Wait what? You have to go.
Please don't mommy! Oh no, oh no.
The teacher says sit in a chair
What are we even doing here?
Learning our letters, days of the week
Reading books, playing hide and seek
Build a tower that's really tall!
Play pretend like I'm taking a call
There's so much to do here, this is a blast
Oh mommy's back, that was fast!
I met some new friends and enjoyed in play
Mommy can I come back another day?

My Store Trip

I want the ball! The train! Ooh a car!
Don't run away! You're going too far.
I am EXCITED! Do you see all the toys?
Why is the pink car not for boys?
I am not out of control. I am exploring the store.
I want books. I want toys. I want candy galore!
Now I am upset. You are telling me no.
We cannot have that and it's time to go.
I'm not spoiled! Just explain to me.
Where you see tears, I'm learning emotionally.
Look at your cart full of good stuff!
When you tell me no, my emotions get rough.
I need help, I do not understand.
Just look at me, take my hand.
Mommy, help know that it's okay.
Explain to me why we cant get it today.

Too Small

Pick me up mommy, it's too high!
If I could, I'd jump up and fly
I need your help mommy I can't reach.
Ugh I'm upset and let out a screech!
I'm so little, I can't wait to grow
I wish they would put more things down low
I know what to do! Grab a chair.
It'll make me higher so I can reach up there.
Look at me! I am so tall!
I have to be careful so I don't fall.
But I can reach it! Look at me!
I am big now! I can see.
I did it myself. Hip hip hooray!
I still can't wait to be big one day.

Food

I don't want chicken. I'm not in the mood.
But I'm still hungry. Please give me food.
Red sauce and noodles. What are these round
things on top?
I tried to play catch with them but mommy told
me to stop.
Meatballs hmmm.. I'll give it a try
Oooo these would be delicious with some
French fries!
I don't think I like Brussels sprouts anymore.
Why is it slippery? Oops onto the floor.
Can I have crackers? They're always the best!
Mmm and a warm glass of milk to put me to
rest.

Outside

Do you hear the crickets? The birds in the tree?
Ooo look around? What do I see?
Mommy what is that? It's a Rollie Pollie!
That black and yellow bug is a bumblebee!
Hey look in the dirt, bugs crawling all around!
Oooo look over here! Look what I found!
Bunnies are going in a burrow in the ground.
Wait! Mommy, what is that sound?
That's a woodpecker. He's way up high!
Look up in the tree, up toward the sky.
Hello there! Who is that guy?
He's a stranger. Just a man walking by.
Look there's a squirrel up in the tree!
And something in the sky! What could it be?
Mommy it's an airplane! Can you see?
Hurry mommy look before it's gone behind the
tree!
Let's run mommy, it makes me feel free
Look! Those flowers are as pretty as can be!
Look at the lake, so pretty and blue.
Mommy I love going outside with you.
There's always something fun to do
Do you love going outside with me too?

My Favorite Swing

I have a favorite swing
It's a small yellow thing
Nothing special but it's mine
If anyone takes it, I'll whine
It's the same as the swing on the right
But my swing touches the sunlight!
When I swing up in the air,
I feel all my problems disappear
I love my swing and everyone knows.
Want to see how high it goes?
I always hold on tight so I won't fall
Mommy please push me, give it your all!
One two three.. push off… big swing!
Nothing compares to how much joy swinging
brings!

Rocks in a Well

I see a well, with water in the ground.
Look around, there's rocks to be found.
We need big ones to make a good splash!
But don't look away it happens in a flash.
The bigger the rocks the louder the sound
Keep an eye out and look all around
I have a handful of rocks to go in the well!
3.. 2.. 1.. drop! All the rocks fell
Ooo listen… Splish! Splash! Plop!
This is so fun, I never want to stop.

Little

I am little, but not for long
Before you know it, I'll sing songs
Count to 10. 1.. 2.. 3..
And I'll know my ABCs
I'll say new words each and every day
My big imagination will show through play
I'll do things that are brand new
And I'll want to show them to you
Put on my pants and tie my shoe
Cut the paper and stick with glue
Run so fast, climb and swing
I will have questions about everything
I am little, but not for long
I'll grow big and get real strong
I learn and grow really fast
Enjoy my little days while they last

Cook With Me

Yum! Potatoes, carrots, and celery
Come along and cook with me
Wash our hands so we can cook
What's to eat? Let's take a look
Pot roast tonight. Mmmmmm delish!
Get the food, oven bag, and the dish
Unwrap and season the veggies and meat
Once it's done you're in for a treat
Now put all the food in the oven bag
I'm a very good cook, I don't mean to brag
On your tongue the flavors will dance
You'll be ready to eat at first glance
In the oven the food goes
Get ready to smell deliciousness with your nose!
We have to be patient until the food is hot
How much time is left? Not a lot.
A few more minutes and "Ding!" goes the bell
Is the food done? Time to tell
Mommy pulls it out and it looks great!
I cannot wait until she makes my plate.

My Dog

My dog is big! He loves to play
If he could, he would fetch all day.
He loves to run! He is very fast.
If we raced I would come in last.
He needs a leash so he won't run away
He has a crate where he likes to lay
He knows how to roll over, sit, and bark
His favorite place is the dog park
He's white and fluffy like a giant bear
He makes me feel safe when he is near
I love my dog! He is my best friend
Right by my side until the days end.

Bubble Bath

Take off my clothes and start the tub.
I've played all day and need a scrub.
Look at my feet, there's dirt on my toes
And dirt on my fingers, arms, and nose
I love the bath, get clean and play
I could splash in bubbles all day
Warm water with toys is the best;
It's very relaxing and good before rest.
In the water, I'd stay if I could.
Mmm these bubbles smell really good!
Now I'm clean! My bath is done.
I can't wait for tomorrow, that bath was fun.
Where's my towel? I need to get dry!
Time to leave the bathroom. I tell my toys bye.

Bedtime

Tuck me in, turn off the light.
Don't go far, I'm easy to fright
Listen mommy, hear that sound?
Oh no! What's moving on the ground?
What's the dark climbing up the wall?
Mommy I'm afraid of it all!
I cannot sleep without you near.
You keep me safe from what I fear.
Hold me mommy, it's such a scary night.
It's too dark. Please turn on the light.
Can we play music to drown out the noise?
Let's clean up and move all of the toys.
No more sounds. No more shadows. Mommy's
right here!
I feel safe. I feel comfy. No longer in fear

Time Flies

Take a breath, breathe with me
Don't take life so seriously
Slow down a bit, have some fun
Who cares what time things get done
Go your pace, enjoy your day
Take time out to laugh and play
Let's be silly or play pretend
Sing a song with no end
Build and create something new
Make some cake and eat it too!
The chores can wait another day
Don't worry they won't go away
Let's live life, don't you stress
There's always going to be a mess!